From Boy
to Man

Poems by Colin Kirkwood

WP
BOOKS

Published by Word Power Books 2015

43–45 West Nicolson Street
Edinburgh
EH8 9DB

www.word-power.co.uk

Cover image Death of a Saltcoats Sandcastle, Bob Lees.

Printed and bound by Bell and Bain Ltd.

Designed by Nicola Regan, Submarine Design.

British Library and Cataloguing in Publication Data.

A catalogue record of this book is available from the
British Library.

ISBN 978-0-9927392-7-0

Most of these poems were previously published in
Nik, 16 Poems, Scottish Poetry, Feedback, Scottish
International, The Scotsman, May, Masque, and
Four Glasgow University Poets, or broadcast on BBC
Radio Scotland. This is the first time they have been
published together as a collection.

Thanks to Bob Lees for permission to reproduce
his fine painting 'Death of a Saltcoats Sandcastle',
to Rachel Kirkwood for help with word processing,
and to Nicky Regan of Submarine Design for
outstanding graphic design and layout.

For good feedback, thanks to Gerri Kirkwood,
Nicky Regan, Robyn Marsack and Hamish Whyte.
And for their generous endorsements, thanks to
Tom Leonard, Bob Tait and Zinnie Harris.

This book is dedicated to my wife Gerri,
our children Paul and Anna, and their children:
Rachel, Peter, David, Sean and Stella.

Contents

Introduction   *10*

What would you do?   *12*

Often I think   *13*

A version of Recueillement   *14*

Baudelaire   *15*

Longing   *16*

Sailing towards Arran   *17*

Boy with red sleeping bag and banana   *18*

A version of An hendy hap   *19*

The green burst buds   *20*

Why is the grass so wet?   *21*

Game   *22*

Boats   *23*

Poem sad   *24*

The Shetland island of Mousa   *25*

Waves   *26*

Today, haze   *27*

Do you want it?   *28*

A kind of loving   *29*

For Jan   *30*

Homage to David Stephen   *31*

Flying upside down   *32*

That pigeon   *34*

Crocuses   *35*

Puss not purring   *36*

Shleepy   *37*

Speakers   *38*

    1   Hallo
    2   Now
    3   If you
    4   She said I stood
    5   O Philip was sure

Landing   *43*

Moving pictures of the wind   *44*

Heavy   *45*

The bin and the bucket   *46*

Gently   *47*

Roadsong   *48*

After a shower   *49*

News item   50

Tiny starman   51

Sunbrite   52

Express breaks news to wife   53

Night special   54

Cloud   55

Round   56

Scene constructing   57

Imagist poem   58

Woods   59

Down inside   60

Latenight   61

Mother and child   62

My trail doesn't exist now   63

In a café (desperately)   64

Face   65

Saint   66

Papyrus   67

Three versions of Eugenio Montale   68

    1   The window
    2   Dawn
    3   Hitler Spring

Storie di Cristo   72

    1   This is a hollow mountain
    2   Jesus up to his chest
    3   Jesus looks worried
    4   All the helmeted soldiers
    5   Jesus carries the cross
    6   Small angels swarming
    7   The soldiers are sleeping
    8   This is the happy ending

Other paintings of the same period   75

    1   The crowning of the virgin
    2   A man sitting on a throne

Confession is good for the hole   76

Two versions of revolution   77

    1   Peace, bread, land
    2   I've just written a letter

Spotted   78

Biography   80

Introduction

It's a strange feeling, sitting down to write an introduction to a collection of poems, the earliest of which were written over fifty years ago.

I left Saltcoats and Ardrossan Academy to go to Glasgow University in the autumn of 1961, at the age of seventeen. I found the teaching of European History uninspiring, and dropped it. But English and Scottish Literature, and Moral Philosophy, with Edwin Morgan, Jack Rillie and William Maclagan, lit fires that are still burning.

I started writing poetry myself, gradually finding my own voice and themes, many of which prefigure the work I've been involved in ever since, in adult education and community action, counselling and psychoanalytic psychotherapy.

The poets whose work I loved most, in those early years, were W B Yeats and Gerard Manley Hopkins. I often got to sleep by reading one or more of Hopkins's dramatic poems of despair, a paradoxical source of comfort. I still recommend them to my psychotherapy clients today.

Other influences included jazz poetry, the folk songs of Leadbelly, Ewan MacColl, Hamish Henderson and others, the poems of Kenneth White, with whom I shared a love of Fairlie Moor and the Firth of Clyde. Another breath of fresh air was the poetry of D H Lawrence.

Thanks to Bob Tait, I found and followed the work of Ian Hamilton Finlay, from The Dancers Inherit the Party, through Poor. Old. Tired. Horse. to concrete poetry and the garden at Stonypath.

Robert Creeley was a big influence. I admired the work of Edwin Morgan, and it was Eddie who drew my attention to the objectivist and imagist traditions in America, particularly to William Carlos Williams, Louis Zukofsky and George Oppen.

Later, while working in Italy, I discovered the poetry of Eugenio Montale. Of the Scottish Renaissance poets I particularly admired Hugh MacDiarmid, Sorley MacLean and Robert Garioch.

Through and around all this was Ezra Pound, whose fascism and anti-semitism disfigured his contributions. A master of modes and voices, a daring translator, a brilliant imagist, a connection-maker defying disciplinary boundaries, at his best Pound transcends his own defects. He juxtaposes modernism, medievalism, classicism and archaism, searching back through time and cultures for sources of wisdom, and challenging us to *make it new*.

That's the context. Out of it, from an awareness of how words can *enact* meanings and relations, and from engagement with my own issues, a personal synthesis emerges. I'll let the poems speak for themselves. They feel as alive now as they did when I wrote them.

Colin Kirkwood, Autumn 2015.

What would you do if I woke up one morning and refused to be me?

Just refused to be Kirkwood, repudiated all my days and mornings, decided to be a spaceman, Biffo the Bear, something like that.

What would you do? What would you really do?

Mother said nothing, just kept on doing whatever it was she was doing.

In fact, Mother wasn't there at all, and if she had been, she would have said:

Stop talking nonsense, for goodness sake, can't you be sensible, some of the daft things you come out with!

I'm beginning to question the wisdom of bringing Mother into this at all.

But what if I did, Mother?

Oh, you, like your Father, persisting! That would be the stupid thing to do! You couldn't do that! Nobody would let you!

But absent irrelevant Mother! I didn't ask for a moral judgement. I asked for a straight answer. What would you do? Nothing!

Christ, think of that. Start off being an elephant and nobody does a thing about it. Just sit there and take it!

often I think a thought that shakes me sober
hell's chief umbrella man am I
I'll shield your head against the sky of summer
and if you ask me why I'll make you cry

A version of Baudelaire's Recueillement

sadness, sadness
cry for darkness
look it's coming
covering you

sea of darkness covering the town

the harsh
day people of the streets
– they look so gay –
pile up
regrets

your little white hand
in my hand
we pick
little flowers

baudelaire wrote poems about women and
cats I
wish that bloody elephant wd   S
                                          T
                                          O
                                          P
                      dancing on the windowledge

longing for the long, lost summer

the galloper on the back of the lonely behind

Sailing towards Arran.

Brodick Bay opens to let you in.

The hills try to speak, but cannot.

Silently embracing you all.

Boy with red sleeping bag and banana
climbs the stairs colourfully.

Everything else is colourful,
each in its own way.

He doesn't notice any other colours.

Banisters run up one set of stairs,
then turn,
then run on, and finally vanish into the wall.

Suddenly he realises
what a convenient thing the staircase is.

A version of the Middle English poem
An hendy hap

A lucky thing has happened to me
it must've been God's doing.
I don't love every girl I see
just Alison.

The green burst buds are heavy and innocent,
like a clear-eyed woman,
carrying a child in her body.
The rain is on them.

I have wrapped my head among them.
I have lived like a present dream.

why is the grass so wet, so wet
the green the grass
he sat in a puddle
up to his middle
and never was seen, and never was seen

Game

she like a bird
flies
at the window

three taps
& the door
three knocks

like a frantic
bird · her father
goes heavily to the
                    door

boats

we

sail

water   sails

past

us

water

stills

sails

us

Poem sad

He shines sad music on his sad guitar,
plays runs, the sad light
rubs on his brow and nose and cheek
as he lones by the window.
The strings' sad notes shine,
might be sad to rub each other.

The Shetland island of Mousa is
uninhabited and is a nature lovers'
paradise, teeming with nesting
sea birds and seals

– and is paradise uninhabited?

– is a mousa shetland sea
island nesting teeming lovers
with the birds and seals of nature?

waves

wavers

rivers

grass

today, haze

the farms of thirdpart
a brown sea

white and dark
smudges of
boats

the road down
to the
sea,
white and blue
blue-white

do you want it
so much,
see her
from afar, how
soft, how bright, but
the soft silence then
is not
between us, rather between
us, how
nice, how
safe is
this self in
its halo world

A kind of loving

when she
asks me, I
sing
to myself, for
myself, for my
gay mirror
lover

For Jan

it has to be something
not to take from
but feed, or give to,
watching wishfully
to see if it grows,
if it will go,
row
us
away

Homage to David Stephen

larger than a rock dove; it was

                            I had

bee-eater. It was not much

          It was my first little

a brown bird with light buff

a bittern

bittern,

strange bird. It flew like a

Flying upside down

It's raining wet, it's raining dry,
the rain is raining to the sky,
the sky is high, the sky is blue,
the boat doth float, and I do too.

Below my head, above my head,
the sky goes *down* – or *up* instead.

The white boat sails me like a cloud…
the falling *silence* seems so *loud*
– the white boat sails me like a kite,
the *heavy* silence seems so *light*.

The falling silence is a concept
of complex reference, like a precept.

(This is the philosophical bit
where I hit things to make them fit.)

The falling silence is a notion
elephantine, like *the ocean.*

It don't just say – there's something there.
It says – you know there's someone here.

(The last two lines, which follow these,
buzz round the elephant like bees.)

Heeheeheeheeheeheehee
memememememememe.

That pigeon in the rain,
sitting in a drain;

stuck onto the roof's straight line,
it may be its, it isn't mine:

in the window uneven thick
the pigeon squirms from slim to thick:

object, object, in a pane,
not-my pigeon, twisting in its rain.

crocuses I saw as a glow
as I left her
just now as
my now her here there

Puss not purring

yellow eyes
        either side of
                the stem of a tulip

the leaves that
        curl from its base
             – green whiskers

the petals crown
        him solemn king
             of the vase

Shleepy

sits, almost
asleep, a
sheep – he follows
the quiet
grass

Speakers

1

hallo
wir back
w'nivir win'in
look
a'v go' a tan
look look
still wurkin
a
iss a shame
see ya

2

now
w'll let some air in
at this one

– j'see that, boy
bluebells
that grow all over
the place

escalonia

turkscap, byu'iful

taste that – it has a nice taste
tirrific, ah
celery
celery,
tirrific

the turkscaps,
tirrific, ah

3

if you
ever pop
up in
the noo
world, please
contact me. I like
you. What I
wanted
to say

4

she said I stood
on a pin in a shop
today that shop aiming
a finger at the dress on the ironing board
some shops
th' pick thim up with a magnit like
jew rimembir that shop
in Buchanan Street w'went t'git a dress'n a coat
fur the wedding that
fat lady rimembir all
her pins dropped'n the floor'n
I started
t'pick thim up'n she
said deunt bothe we
gaathe thim ole it thee end iv the dehy
withe megnit

5

O Philip was sure th'would *pile* int'the dance

    O a *few* came
    but *very* few
    fewer'n ex*pect*ed

O what can y'ex*pect*?
We told'm not t'*count*
the ones that weren't comin'

    O the *dance*!
    the *dance* wuz
    a good *dance*!

Landing

hugeous tree! hovers
over the field

heads of grass and weeds
look up

– and
down!

shakes itself,
like a leafy hen

what an odd tree:
it's gone to sleep – standing up!

Moving pictures of the wind

swiftswift
     slow
         crow

trees
   stand in air!

the wind blows
       noises,
           blows *noses*!

heavy

water

drips

water

drops

drops

lips

The bin and the bucket

the bin and the bucket
round and grey
side by side
day by day

both are
cylindrical
but the bucket
is upside down

garbage containers
is what they are
but the bin men
never come

to take the contents away
so day by day
contents
accumulate around them

the bin
is full
and the bucket
is upside down

gently

the

bananas

fish

no

water

how

trying

Roadsong

up a long
rising road
saying you're
lost saying
this road is
a vague con
tinuity
a line you
go up a
sense of it

a long wry singing

After a shower

blue whales lie
in the big white sky
teardrops of rain
(not falling) (on the pane) are
still small grey'n white
fish out of water

News item

the 8$\frac{1}{2}$ lb
man with
bright
red feet –
his
he-dragon
almost
unnoticed –
will go
tonight
home to
his scottish
basket

TINY STARMAN MISSING

LOST IN FADES OF SNOW SKY

sunbrite

STAR

BLUE ANGELS OK

for your wedding car

EXPRESS BREAKS NEWS TO WIFE
TO EXPRESS WIFE, BREAKS NEWS
TO EXPRESS NEWS, BREAKS WIFE
EXPRESS BREAKS WIFE TO NEWS

NIGHT SPECIAL

NIGHT SAFE

night night

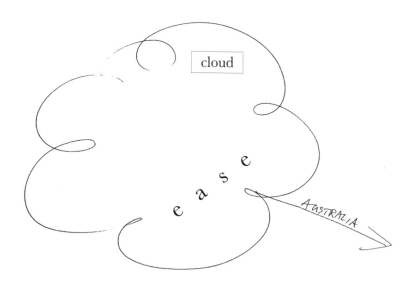

round

ponds

and

rods

Scene constructing

white paper
water

slopes taper
depth

eye elopes with
cows that saunter up
towards other cows

during the interval
waiting
for the next item to
start up

haze
drifts
hills

clouds
start up...

Imagist poem

The carrier of the potato-sack's
large arse

distends his coat which
extends to his feet.

He runs in my mind
slowly on his feet.

woods
that seemed away sadly
out of reach, out of touch…
on the beach, we
as kids dug damp grey
holes, bowls that seep
fill
through the bottom, reverse sieve-process…
we seemed
outside process, looking on,
not ingredient, inside
the house, too…

Down inside

firtree leaning
loning one side
vertical grey
way up out to
blue sky high barred
by bars stand hard
straight trunks push bush
blue high from you

Latenight

on a side road, co
incident black
tracks in the snow

icing, pavement, wedge
up: black steeple aims high

sportscar, zip!
red stars enter the
black clearway!

Mother and child

looking from the door, a chair's in the road
you can see her small face
                    small breasts   air-triangle

a red table-top
paves a different approach

scene composed
of functional objects,
incidentally
a mother and child

a wooden angle
poise on the table
Pinnocchio
bowed low

My trail doesn't exist now. I walked it. Don't
forget the butter, we do need it, to seal mouse-holes
in the skirting-board, the mice lick through,
we need butter again, we introduced the mice ourselves,
not out of love, but something to do. The trail was
marked by clashes, of feet and pavement, heard as going.
In passing, a dive-view of space underground:
pub-cellar. The pavement is a hard roof.

We get married on Saturdays, mostly, in a white
dress. Ach, a long day tomorrow. That this cup
might pass from me. We work furiously, subside
like burst tyres.

in a cafe (desperately)
trying to take off into sound-track film

espresso, the coffee swings in the cup

light-bulb on side under table
where feet settle

Face

as lying in bed
sensations embed,
grow sore

so I see
my face in mirrors

the mask
of flesh and skin
thickening,

performer
of grimaces, smiles, etc

sometimes I let go
the quiet tense across grip

show an early form
of an old lady's:

grooved dependent, holey

Saint

Jerome, fat
belly, books
to left and/right
hand on the page, the
sun/behind his hat

Papyrus

Love awaits me
over the river,
also a fucking
crocodile.
Nevertheless, I shall resolutely
walk across,
firm as terra under my feet.
Your love, my love,
gives me this power.
When I see you
I jump up and down
and open arms wide
to enfold you.

Three versions of poems by Eugenio Montale

1   A version of *Il Balcone*

The window

It should've been child's play to
turn into next-to-nothing the
newly-opened space, you
into tiresome words. But

here space-you comes through
my slow efforts, here the
effort of living with you's
stuck. Trips to the wreck.

You can see glimmerings
of a lighter life. I can see you
looking out this unlit
window towards it.

2   A version of *Lungomare*

Dawn

wind freshening, darkness
paling. Your shadow's dark
on the pailings. Too late to be

your self alone. A mouse jumps down
out of your sleeve, slips into
a slit in the kerb.

3   A version of *La Primavera Hitleriana*

Hitler Spring

Hitler and Mussolini in Florence
On the Arno, a snowstorm of butterflies

Dense white cloud of maddened moths
whirls round the misted headlights, and the guardrails:
on the ground, matting your feet would crunch on
like on sugar. Now imminent summer
sets free night-frost kept
in secret caverns of the dead season,
in the orchards stretching from Maiano to these sands.

A few minutes ago, one of hell's couriers sped along the main road
through heils of nazis, a misty abyss
lit by swastikas swallowed him up.
Shop windows've been shuttered, poor inoffensive
things – though armed themselves with
rifles and other battle toys.
The butcher's shut – the bloke that used to
decorate the slaughtered goats' snouts by sticking twigs through them.
The rite of the gentle killers ignoring the blood
gives place to a terrified collusion; larvae, the river
gnawing away at the banks, broken wings.
No-one can plead not guilty.

So all for nothing? The roman candles
in the church of San Giovanni, that slowly made the horizon
glow, the promises, the long farewells,
strong as baptisms, in the loving purgatory of waiting
for them to arrive (but a gem of rain
hits the ground, Tobias' angel, a seed
of the future), and the heliotropes you
nurtured – all sucked and burnt up
by a flower that thunders like a big fire,
a sandstorm…

Spring will be spring
when we've killed this killer. (We who changed
make love unchanged.) *He* won't change
till the blind sun in each of us *sees* the other,
and shines for them. Maybe the sirens and bells that
announce the parades and displays these evenings have already
been laced with the sound that, loosed from heaven,
will land and save – with the breath of a dawn that tomorrow
will shine for all, white without wings
of terror, on the burnt-up riverbeds of the south.

Storie di Cristo

14th century paintings by Paolo da Venezia

1

This is a hollow mountain
a tent.
In it a cradle and in it the baby,
shining.
A cow is licking his right arm.
A donkey is licking his left ear.
The audience is wearing crowns, halos, wings,
or at least praying.
He's got his eye on the cow.

2

Jesus up to his chest in green water.
Red-haired John the Baptist
reaches a skinny arm from the bank
to touch his head. Towards it
a pigeon bombing straight down
from the blue sun.
Talk about vertical take-off!

3

Jesus looks worried at the head of the table
(halo bigger than the rest).
He's got a hand on John's shoulder.
Eleven of the twelve have halos.
They're looking at him, or at each other,
worriedly.
Judas is sitting on a stool
not on the bench like the rest.
No halo, hair uncombed,
reaching for a piece of bread or fish.
He looks at Jesus, feeling: *he knows*.

4

All the helmeted soldiers
are watching Judas kiss Jesus
but the eyes of these two
have flicked left:
Peter is sawing off this bloke's ear.

5

Jesus carries the cross effortlessly
flashing a worried glance
back at his mother –
who's gone all emotional
wringing her hands.
The man behind her son
wearing a black dagger
shoves her out of the road.

6

Small angels swarming round the cross,
one is catching the blood in a bowl.
Jesus' eyes are shut.
One of the soldiers is pointing up at him solemnly
and he has a halo.
The rest of them look neutral
like people at the pictures.
But on the left
one of the women has stabbed herself
with a big sword!

7

The soldiers are sleeping.
An angel is standing in the empty coffin.
Mary is asking the gardener:
where's the body?

8

This is the happy ending, supposed to be.
Jesus in a big egg
carried by angels
in mid-air
…head bent
looking down worriedly
at the people on the ground
looking up at him
worriedly.

Other paintings of the same period

1

There are several of the crowning of the virgin
in which Jesus and Mary are side by side on a throne.
Both heads are bent
in pity-love towards each other
but Mary's is *more* bent.
Her curvy form looks boneless.
I guess her lord is saying:
keep it up dear, you're going a grand job,
look, d'you mind if I leave you the dishes tonight,
there's a bloke I promised to wake from the dead…
Lutes, flutes and xylophones
sound all round.

2

A man sitting on a throne in mid air
presumably God. He looks serious.
Down below, lots of skeletons
laughing happily,
holding little red books in their hands.
Mao wasn't the first.

Confession is good for the hole

That makes about two months I haven't
had a bath, washed only face
in the mornings sometimes, when rubbing of eyes
left burny sensation – my prick stinks,
it's not even nice like the seaweed smell of cunt. But
given that today I've buggered myself
looking at Padua, and just gorged
half a bag cherries, and half the plate of exquisite
soup they brought us to try from next door (the other half
being for Gerri, who's across the hall I discover
having curlers put in by the dressmaker), and that the noise
of the bath filling might wake Paul, I've decided to postpone it
again indefinitely. Anyway
I've just finished Morris who suggests
that the frequency of washing in our species cannot be explained
functionally, solely as an anti-disease precaution
(given that we remove with soap and water the oil
the skin produces for just that purpose), but also
as grooming, which presupposes a pleasure content,
or at least habit, neither of which is involved
in my case, as I tend to get depressed
in the bath, not sure why. Anyway
given finally that I've just tried to shit
and failed, and feel that well known blocked
feeling, I'd rather sit down and write a free-flow poem.

Two versions of revolution

1

Peace, bread, land

Lenin, addressing a dense crowd,
raised above them, so each can see him.
They stand. They listen. Together.
He stands. He speaks. Alone.

a plane
shaves off the worn surface of false consciousness,
bares the fresh wood, the integral powers of each of these people.
Today the blade is: peace, bread, land.

2

I've just written a letter to a friend,
full of enthusiasm.
When will the revolution come?
When people make it.

grey pavement
      spotted
            with black rain

green slope
      spotted
            with yellow buttercups

Biography

Colin Kirkwood is a son of the manse who grew up in Caithness, Galloway and Ayrshire. He studied at Ardrossan Academy, the Universities of Glasgow and Edinburgh, and the Scottish Institute of Human Relations. He has been described as a Scottish generalist, with interests in literature and the arts, moral philosophy, politics, education, religion, and psychoanalysis. His working life has been devoted to adult and workers education, community action, and latterly counselling and psychoanalytic psychotherapy. He was WEA District Secretary in south-east Scotland, Senior Lecturer in Counselling Studies at the University of Edinburgh, and Senior Psychotherapist at Huntercombe Hospital, where he worked with women and girls with severe eating disorders.

He is the author of *The Scots as Persons in Transition: there is another way* (2014), *The Persons in Relation Perspective in counselling, psychotherapy and community adult learning* (2012), *Living Adult Education: Freire in Scotland* (with Gerri Kirkwood) (1989, 2007, 2011), *The Development of Counselling in Shetland: a study of counselling in society* (2000), *Vulgar Eloquence: essays on education, community and politics* (1990), *and Adult Education and the Unemployed* (edited, with Sally Griffiths) (1984).

Earlier publications included: *Angelic Talker: an introduction to the poetry of Robert Creeley* (1967), *Community Democracy* (1975) and *Vulgar Eloquence: the poetry of Tom Leonard* (1985).

During the 1970s and 80s, he played a leading part in the community newspaper and writers workshop movements. Publications with which he was associated include *Staveley Now*, *Castlemilk Today*, *Scottish Tenant* and *Clock Work*.